DB PUBLISHING

Copyright © 2023

DB Publishing

All right reserved. No part of this book may be reproduced or used in any manner without the written permission of the copyright owner except for the use of the quotations in a book review.

First Edition 2023

Table of Contents

2 - Information
3 - African Forest Elephant
5 - Amur Leopard
7 - Black Rhino
9 - Bornean Orangutan
11 - Cross River Gorilla
13 - Hawksbill Sea Turtle
15 - Axolotl
17 - Saola (Asian Unicorn)
19 - Iberian Lynx
21 - Sunda Tiger
23 - Vaquita
25 - Sumatran Orangutan (Person of the Forest)
27 - Yangtze Finless Porpoise
29 - Sumatran Rhino
31 - Pangolin
33 - Plains Bison
35 - Polar Bear
37 - Giant Panda
39 - Blue Whale
41 - What You Can Do To Help

Information

You have probably heard the term, endangered species; most people have. What we often don't know is where they typically live, why they are endangered, and what their extinction would cost the planet in terms of why their presence in the world is important.
This book aims to answer those questions.
On each coloring page you'll see one endangered animal along with their name, where they most often live, what is threatening their existence, and either their importance to other life in the world or hopeful information on what is being done to protect them.

Coloring is a form of meditation. Our goal was to create a book for meditative coloring that would also help the person using it to understand a little more about these endangered species. If that person then becomes more of an advocate in the world for the protection of these animals, all the better.

The coloring images are in the form of a mandala. A mandala is a symbol of something in its ideal form; it symbolizes the transformation of suffering into one of joy.
Thank you for purchasing this coloring book. In so doing you are taking one step toward helping these animals continue to live among us on this precious planet. May your coloring experience be peaceful and help you connect to the animals whose images you are bringing to life and whose lives you are bringing to mind.

African Forest Elephant

Location: West and Central Africa
Threatened by poaching for bushmeat and ivory.
Essential for the germination of many rain forest trees.
The seeds of these trees only germinate after passing
through the elephant's digestive tract.

Amur Leopard

Primorye region of southeastern Russia and northern China
Threatened by poaching and prey species.
The ecosystem would become unbalanced and
damage our water, air and land deforestation.

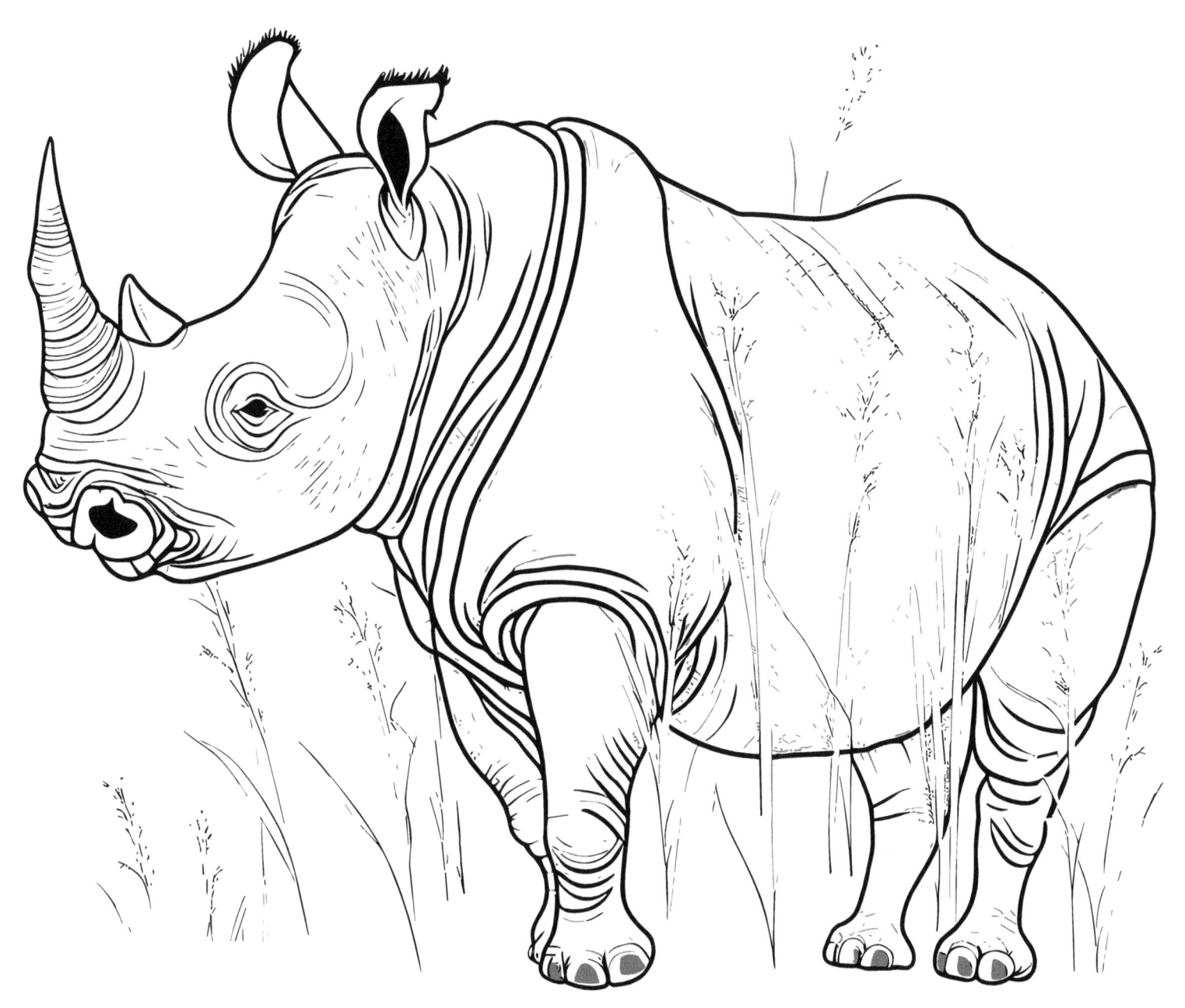

Black Rhino

Southern and eastern Africa, including Kenya, Tanzania, Namibia, South Africa and Zimbabwe
Threatened by poaching.
They are being sedated and flown by helicopter to another place for safety to reproduce.

Bornean Orangutan
Lowland rainforests and tropical, swamp and mountain forests of Sabah and eastern Kalimantan
Threatened by human hunting,
unsustainable and often illegal logging, mining, and conversion of forests to agriculture.
Orangutans play a critical role in seed dispersal, keeping forests healthy.

Cross River Gorilla
Congo Basin

Threatened by humans illegally hunting and killing gorillas. Organizations have established ranger posts, provided field and communication equipment for antipoaching staff, and established a system to monitor the gorilla population.

Hawksbill Sea Turtle

Found throughout the world's tropical oceans, predominantly in coral reefs.
Threatened by fishery-related mortality, pollution, coastal development, but mostly wildlife trade.
They maintain the health of coral reefs by removing prey such as sponges from the reef's surface to provide better access for reef fish to feed.

Axolotl (Peter Pan of Salamanders)
Lakes and canals in the southern part of Mexico City
Threatened by habitat degradation, pollution, fishing, nonnative predators, the pet trade.
They regrow body parts—including their hearts, spines, and brains—and can accept organs and limbs transplanted from other axolotls without risk of rejection, ***medical research.

Saola (Asian Unicorn)

Annamite Mountains of Vietnam and Laos
Threatened by chainsaws to make way for agriculture, plantations and infrastructure which squeezes their areas to thrive. Little is known about how many are left.
The saola is a strong symbol for biodiversity.

Sumatran Elephant

Borneo and Sumatra
Threatened by habitat loss and as a result human-elephant conflict.
They feed on a variety of plants and deposit seeds wherever they go, contributing to a healthy forest ecosystem.

Iberian Lynx

Spain
Threatened by decrease of rabbits, reduction in habitat;
being caught in snares set for rabbits;
accidental deaths caused by speeding vehicles.

Sunda Tiger

Sunda islands in Indonesia
Killed deliberately for commercial gain.
Important indicator of a forest's health and biodiversity - many other species benefit from their existence.

Vaquita

Mexico's Gulf of California
Threatened by entanglement in gillnets.
The most endangered cetacean in the world.
Need fully enforced gillnet ban.

Sumatran Orangutan (Person of the Forest)

Sumatra and further south into Java
Threatened by fire and conversion of forests to oil palm plantations and other agricultural development.
Play a vital role in the dispersal of seeds over a huge area.
Tree species with large seeds would disappear.

Yangtze Finless Porpoise
The Yangtze River, the longest river in Asia. Threatened by overfishing that contributes to the decrease in finless porpoises' food supply, but pollution and ship movement are factors as well. Reconnection of more than 40 floodplain lakes with the main stem of the Yangtze River to restore seasonal flows and allow the migration of species.

Sumatran Rhino
Indonesian islands of Sumatra and Borneo
Threatened by growing consumer demand for rhino horn, degraded by invasive species, road construction, and encroachment for agricultural expansion.
Protecting rhinos helps maintain other animal and plant life in the area and keeps ecosystems healthy.

Pangolin

Africa and Asia
Threatened by being the most trafficked mammal
in the world for their scales and meat;
pangolin products like boots, bags, and belts.

Plains Bison

United States: umbrella species for many plants and animals . US Government tried to eliminate the bison to subdue the Native people that relied upon them. Conservationists and Indigenous peoples brought the plains bison back from the brink of extinction. Bison shaped the landscape. They affect the pattern and structure of the grasses and vegetation. Expansive areas of native grasslands allowed animals to flourish along with many species of other prairie wildlife.

Polar Bear

The largest bear in the world and the Arctic's top predator.
Threats: loss of sea ice habitat from climate change,
lethal response to human-polar bear conflict,
toxic pollution, industrial development
causing oil spills, and potential overhunting.
Polar bears are at the top of the food chain and have an
important role in the overall health of the marine environment.

Giant Panda
Mountains of southwest China,
where they subsist almost entirely on bamboo.
Threatened by infrastructure development which
fragments and isolates pandas preventing pandas from
finding bamboo forests and potential mates.
Biological diversity: when we protect pandas, we protect
other animals such as multicolored pheasants,
the golden monkey, takin, and crested ibis.

Blue Whale

Chile, Arctic, The Galápagos, Coral Triangle, Coastal East Africa

Despite moratorium, Iceland, Japan, and Norway continue commercial whale hunts. Collisions with ships, entanglement in fishing gear (known as bycatch), and pollution injure and kill whales.

Whales play a significant role in capturing carbon from the atmosphere; each great whale sequesters about 33 tons of CO_2, thus fighting against climate change.

What Can You Do To Help

No Plastic in Nature

Protect Birds and Bees

Support the Tropical Deforestation-free Procurement Act

Commit to a Livable and Just Climate Future

Pledge for Our Planet

Extended Producer Responsibility (US only)

Stop Wildlife Crime

Help Stop Future Pandemics (US Only)

Protect Tigers by Switching to Forest-Friendly Products

National Endangered Species Day, May 19th

www.ingramcontent.com/pod-product-compliance
Lightning Source LLC
LaVergne TN
LVHW072132060526
838201LV00072B/5018